YOUR PASSPORT TO

ENGLAND

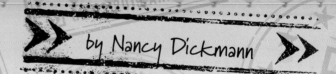

by Nancy Dickmann

CONTENT CONSULTANT

Aidan Forth, PhD
Associate Professor, History
MacEwan University

CAPSTONE PRESS
a capstone imprint

Published by Capstone Press, an imprint of Capstone
1710 Roe Crest Drive, North Mankato, Minnesota 56003
capstonepub.com

Library of Congress Cataloging-in-Publication Data
Names: Dickmann, Nancy, author.
Title: Your passport to England / by Nancy Dickmann.
Description: North Mankato, Minnesota : Capstone Press, an imprint of Capstone, [2022] | Series: World passport | Includes bibliographical references and index. | Audience: Ages 8-11 | Audience: Grades 4-6 | Summary: "What is it like to live in or visit England? What makes England's culture unique? Explore the geography, traditions, and daily lives of England's people"-- Provided by publisher.
Identifiers: LCCN 2021028699 (print) | LCCN 2021028700 (ebook) | ISBN 9781663959270 (hardcover) | ISBN 9781666321920 (paperback) | ISBN 9781666321937 (pdf) | ISBN 9781666321951 (kindle edition)
Subjects: LCSH: England--Juvenile literature. | Great Britain--History--Juvenile literature.
Classification: LCC DA27.5 .D53 2022 (print) | LCC DA27.5 (ebook) | DDC 942--dc23
LC record available at https://lccn.loc.gov/2021028699
LC ebook record available at https://lccn.loc.gov/2021028700

Editorial Credits
Editor: Marie Pearson; Designer: Colleen McLaren; Production Specialists: Christine Ha and Laura Manthe

Image Credits
Red Line Editorial, 5; Shutterstock: Aniczkania, 24, Anna Mente, 20, Christopher Hotton, 14, Cosmin Iftode, 27, duncan1890, 9, Filip Bjorkman, Cover, Flipser, (passport) design element, Helen Hotson, 13, ian woolcock, 6, Kurt Pacaud, 23, MicroOne, (visa stamps) design element, Mr Nai, Cover, Nick Brundle Photography, 29, Noppasin Wongchum, Cover, Pack-Shot, 19, Pecold, 15, PHOTOCREO Michal Bednarek, 16, pingebat, (stamps) design element, Yevhenii Dubinko, (stamps) design element

All internet sites appearing in back matter were available and accurate when this book was sent to press.

Printed and bound in the United States of America.   PO4608

CONTENTS

Words in **bold** are in the glossary.

CHAPTER ONE

WELCOME TO ENGLAND!

Tall stone blocks reach toward the sky. Many stones stand upright. They are about 13 feet (4 meters) high. Some of them are topped by flat stones. The stones form a circle. Green fields stretch all around. This is Stonehenge in England. It was built thousands of years ago. It is one of the oldest and most famous landmarks in England.

England is a country in Europe. It is on the island of Great Britain. England is part of the United Kingdom. Three other countries are also part of the United Kingdom. They are Scotland, Wales, and Northern Ireland. England is the biggest of the four. Each country has its own identity, but they all work together.

MAP OF ENGLAND

N W E S

- ■ Capital City
- ● City
- ▲ Landmark
- ★ Park
- ◆ Attraction

Hadrian's Wall

Fountains Abbey

Liverpool

Manchester

Sherwood Forest

Cambridge

Gloucester

Oxford

LONDON

Bath

Stonehenge

Bodiam Castle

Jurassic Coast

Salisbury Cathedral

Explore England's cities and landmarks.

Boats are important for England's fishing villages.

SURROUNDED BY SEA

Sailing is important for the island nation. Early **invaders** arrived by boat. Later, the country built a powerful **navy**. It protected the British **Empire**. Boats brought **immigrants** from many countries. Now, ferries and underwater train tunnels carry passengers. Fishing boats cast their nets.

FACT FILE

OFFICIAL NAME: .... ENGLAND
POPULATION: 56,286,961
LAND AREA: .... 50,313 SQ. MI. (130,311 SQ KM)
CAPITAL: .... LONDON
MONEY: .... BRITISH POUND
GOVERNMENT: .... PARLIAMENTARY CONSTITUTIONAL MONARCHY
LANGUAGE: .... ENGLISH
GEOGRAPHY: England shares the island of Great Britain with Scotland and Wales. Northern Ireland shares an island with the Republic of Ireland. This island lies across the Irish Sea to the west. France is south, across the English Channel.
NATURAL RESOURCES: England has coal, petroleum, and gas. Farmers grow wheat, barley, oats, and vegetables such as potatoes. Fishing is an important industry.

PEOPLE AND LANGUAGE

Many people have moved to England. Some came from lands the United Kingdom once ruled. These people brought their languages and cultures. English is the main language. It developed in England. It is now the most widely used language in the world.

CHAPTER TWO

HISTORY OF ENGLAND

The first Britons settled in present-day England about 12,000 years ago. At first, they hunted. Then they began to grow crops and raise animals. They set up Stonehenge and other stone circles.

FACT

In the 800s, Alfred the Great united a large area of England. Before then, several kings ruled small areas.

Many people have either invaded or immigrated to England. The Romans came in 55 **BCE**. They built roads and **aqueducts**. Next came the Saxons, Vikings, and Normans.

England has been ruled by many kings and queens. Henry VIII reigned from 1509 to 1547 **CE**. His daughter Elizabeth I reigned from 1558 to 1603.

Queen Elizabeth I was an influential monarch.

In 1600, the English East India Company began trading with Asia. The company eventually conquered India. This meant it did not have to compete with other countries for goods. In 1607, English colonists arrived in the Americas. England had **colonies** in what is now the United States until 1776.

In 1707, England and Scotland joined together. They became Great Britain. The many regions under British control were called the British Empire. In some colonies, Great Britain built railroads and hospitals. But the British also often mistreated local people. A famine hit part of India in 1770. A famine is a lack of food. It killed millions of people. It was so deadly because the British did not store enough food. They sold it all for profit.

In the 1700s, the Industrial Revolution began. This period lasted into the 1800s. **Steam engines** powered factories and trains. Colonies in the Americas, India, and Africa provided materials for England's factories.

In 1801, England and Ireland joined together. The United Kingdom was formed. Queen Victoria reigned from 1837 to 1901. The United Kingdom was the world's most powerful country at this time.

RECENT HISTORY

The United Kingdom was still powerful in the 1900s. It fought in World War I (1914–1918) and World War II (1939–1945).

TIMELINE OF ENGLISH HISTORY

3000 BCE: Early Britons start to set up Stonehenge.

55 BCE: The first Roman soldiers arrive in England.

787 CE: Vikings start to raid settlements in England.

1066: The Normans invade.

1642–1651: Civil war breaks out as King Charles I fights against **Parliament**.

1688–1689: The Glorious Revolution takes place. It results in the Bill of Rights giving more power to Parliament, which is elected by the people.

1757: The East India Company starts governing India.

1914–1918: England fights in World War I.

1939–1945: England fights in World War II.

1973: The United Kingdom joins what will become the European Union.

2015: Queen Elizabeth II becomes the longest-reigning monarch in English history. She passes Queen Victoria's previous record of 63 years and 7 months.

2016: The United Kingdom votes to leave the European Union.

In 1973, the United Kingdom joined a group of European countries. This group later became the European Union. In 2016, the United Kingdom voted to leave the European Union. Today, England still has a monarch. But the prime minister is the head of government.

CHAPTER THREE

EXPLORE ENGLAND

Gently rolling hills cover much of England. In the north, there are hills and mountains. An area called the Lake District has the country's highest peaks. Lakes nestle between the mountains. Their calm surfaces reflect the sky.

England has a long coastline. No place in England is more than 70 miles (113 kilometers) from the sea. In the northeast, the coast is flat and sandy. In Cornwall in the southwest, it is rocky and steep. Part of the southern coast is called the Jurassic Coast. The sea is wearing away its crumbling cliffs. Many fossils have been discovered there.

SHERWOOD FOREST

Long ago, large parts of England were covered in forests. Many of them have been cut down for farmland, but some remain. Sherwood Forest is one of the most famous. According to legend, Robin Hood once lived here. Today, the forest is protected.

Cornwall has beautiful coasts. It has a warmer climate than the rest of England.

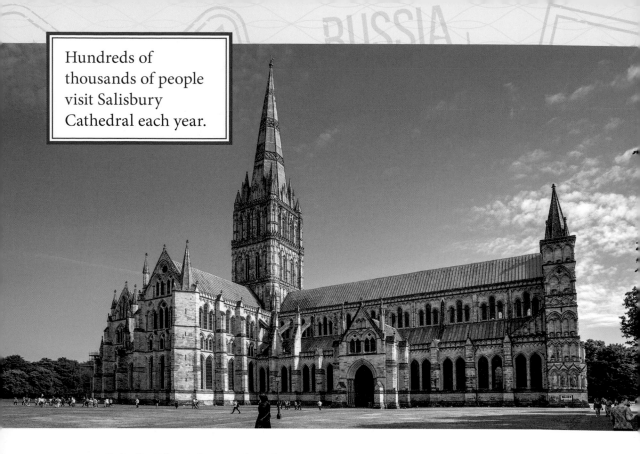

Hundreds of thousands of people visit Salisbury Cathedral each year.

CASTLES AND CATHEDRALS

There are castles all over England. Many are hundreds of years old. Bodiam Castle is one popular castle. It was built in the 1300s.

There are grand churches too. Many are hundreds of years old. Salisbury Cathedral is the tallest church in England. Its spire is 404 feet (123 m) high. A spire is a tall, tapering structure at the top of a church or tower. York Minster has beautiful stained-glass windows.

The Roman Baths get water from nearby hot springs.

Monks once lived at Fountains Abbey. Now, only the walls remain. It is a peaceful place for a picnic.

ROMAN REMAINS

Some sites date back to Roman times. Hadrian's Wall was built in 122 CE. It kept out invaders from Scotland. Large parts of it remain. The city of Bath has an ancient Roman bathhouse. People once believed the water in the bathhouse was good for health.

The UK government meets in the Houses of Parliament (left). The bell in the clock tower is called Big Ben.

BUSY CITIES

London is England's capital. It is also the biggest city. The River Thames flows through the center. Historic buildings line the river's banks. Bridges connect the two sides. People from all over the world live in London. There are restaurants, shops, offices, and museums.

Liverpool is in the northwest. People there once built large ships that crossed the Atlantic Ocean. In the 1700s, some of these ships transported enslaved people from Africa to colonies in North and South America.

FACT

Tower Bridge stands across the Thames in London. It was completed in 1894. Its road deck is a drawbridge. The sides lift up so tall ships can pass through.

Manchester is east of Liverpool. In the past, cloth was made in its mills. Now, many of these buildings have been turned into homes.

CHAPTER FOUR

DAILY LIFE

England is densely populated. Most people live in towns and cities. They often travel on double-decker buses. The world's oldest subway system is in London. Other people live in the countryside. Some grow crops, such as wheat and barley, on small farms. Many people work in offices, shops, and restaurants.

FACT

More than 14 percent of people in England were born in a different country.

EDUCATION

Most children in England start school at the age of 4. They go to primary school for six years. Then they go to secondary school. At most schools, students wear uniforms. Some students go on to study at a university. Oxford and Cambridge have famous universities.

The London Underground subway system is nicknamed the Tube.

Fish-and-chips is commonly served with mushy peas.

FOOD AND DRINK

Fish-and-chips is a popular meal in England. Chips is the British word for french fries. The fish is usually codfish or another whitefish. It is battered and fried.

SCONES

English people are famous for drinking tea. Afternoon tea is often served with cakes, biscuits (cookies), or baked goods such as scones.

Scone Ingredients:
- 2 cups all-purpose flour
- 1 tablespoon powdered sugar
- 1 ½ tablespoons baking powder
- pinch of salt
- 1 cup milk
- 2 tablespoons butter (melted)
- raisins (optional)

Scone Directions:
1. Preheat the oven to 425°F.
2. Mix the flour, powdered sugar, baking powder, and salt in a bowl.
3. Add the milk and butter and stir to combine.
4. Knead the mixture on a floured surface until smooth. Add the raisins if desired.
5. Roll the dough out until it is about 0.5 inch (1 centimeter) thick. Use a round cookie cutter to cut circles 2–3 inches (5–8 cm) in diameter. A drinking glass will also work.
6. Bake for 8–10 minutes, until the scones are golden brown.
7. To serve, split a scone in half and spread with butter or whipped cream and jam.

Roast dinners with meat and vegetables are common. Indian-style curry is also popular. Restaurants serve food from all over the world. People enjoy dishes from Asia, Africa, and the Caribbean.

CHAPTER FIVE

HOLIDAYS AND CELEBRATIONS

People in England have several celebrations each year. People celebrate Bonfire Night on November 5. In 1605, a group of men tried to blow up the Houses of Parliament. This building is also called the Palace of Westminster. Guards stopped them. The king ordered a celebration. Bonfires were lit across the country. Today, people gather to light bonfires and watch fireworks.

Some English events have been taking place for hundreds of years. In May, people near Gloucester chase a wheel of cheese down a steep hill. Most of them fall and tumble down the hill. The first to the bottom wins the cheese. The event has been happening since about the 1400s.

Some people celebrate Bonfire Night with huge bonfires.

RELIGIOUS HOLIDAYS

Christianity is the most common religion in England. Several Christian festivals are celebrated. The main ones are Christmas and Easter.

Many places in England put up light displays for Christmas.

At Christmas, people share gifts and food with family and friends. Some go to church. At Easter, people give large chocolate eggs as gifts. Children have Easter egg hunts. Families gather to share a meal, often roast lamb.

England is home to many Muslims, Hindus, Sikhs, and people of other religions. Hindus and Sikhs celebrate Diwali in the fall. It is a festival of lights. There are candles and fireworks. People share sweet treats. England's Muslims observe Ramadan. It is a month of fasting and prayer. Fasting is giving up certain foods or drinks or eating very little for a period of time. A holiday called Eid al-Fitr celebrates the end of Ramadan. Families gather to share a meal and exchange gifts. They donate food and money to those in need.

ONE BUILDING, MANY FAITHS

The Brick Lane Jamme Masjid is a mosque in East London. It was built in 1743 as a Christian church. In 1898, it became a Jewish synagogue. In 1976, it became a mosque. Muslims still worship there. During Ramadan, evening meals are served each night in the basement.

CHAPTER SIX

SPORTS AND RECREATION

Sports are important in England. Soccer is called football. Soccer is very popular. At matches, spectators chant to support their team. The most successful clubs attract top players from around the world. Teams from all levels can compete in the Football Association Cup. This competition is also called the FA Cup. The men's tournament has been played since 1871. The women's competition has been played since 1970.

There are other popular sports too. Cricket is a bat-and-ball game. It is often played on an oval field. Some matches are a few hours long. Others last for five days. Many people enjoy rugby. Two teams try to run the ball down a field to score points. Girls and women often play netball. This sport is similar to basketball.

People in England enjoy cheering on their favorite soccer teams, including Manchester United.

BRITISH BULLDOG

The game British Bulldog is a children's game played on playgrounds and sports fields across the country. It can be played by groups of any size. There are many versions of the rules.

1. One person is chosen to be the bulldog. If the group is very large, there might be two or three bulldogs.
2. The bulldog stands in the middle of the field. The other players all line up on one side. This is a safe zone. The opposite side of the field is the other safe zone.
3. When the bulldog gives a signal, all the players must run to the other side. The bulldog tries to tag them.
4. Anyone who gets caught becomes a bulldog and joins the original bulldog.
5. The game ends when all the players have been caught.

ARTS AND ENTERTAINMENT

England is known for its many museums. There are art museums in most big cities. The British Museum in London displays treasures from around the world. Other museums teach about science or history. The International Slavery Museum is in Liverpool. It has displays about England's role in the slave trade.

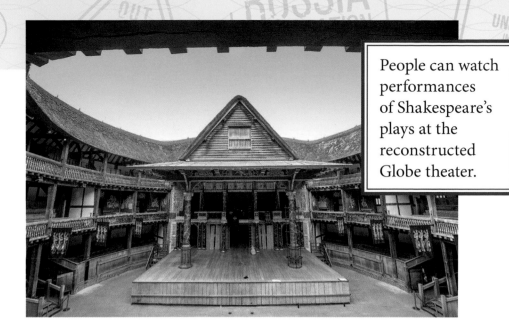

People can watch performances of Shakespeare's plays at the reconstructed Globe theater.

There is a long tradition of theater in England. In the 1600s, William Shakespeare's plays were performed at a London theater called the Globe. In the 1990s, a replica opened. Many famous actors have performed there. London's West End has dozens of theaters. People go to watch comedies, dramas, and musicals.

AN ISLAND JEWEL

England has a rich history. It has beautiful countryside, exciting cities, and historic landmarks. There are fascinating places to explore and delicious foods to try. For a small country, there is a lot to see and do.

GLOSSARY

aqueduct (AWK-wuh-duhkt)
a structure that allows water to flow over rivers or valleys to human settlements

BCE/CE
BCE means Before Common Era, or before year one. CE means Common Era, or the years starting with year one

colony (KAH-luh-nee)
an area that is controlled by a foreign country and where people from that foreign country have settled

empire (EM-pire)
a large area of land, sometimes of multiple territories, ruled over by a single person or group

immigrant (IM-i-gruhnt)
a person who moves to another country to live

invader (in-VAY-duhr)
a person who enters another area and takes control of it

monk (MUNK)
a man who promises to live a simple life dedicated to prayer and good works

navy (NAY-vee)
the branch of a country's armed forces that operates at sea

parliament (PAR-luh-ment)
a group made up of representatives who make laws

steam engine (STEEM EN-jin)
a type of engine that burns coal to heat water, which makes steam to power the engine

READ MORE

Blevins, Wiley. *United Kingdom*. New York: Scholastic, 2018.

Knufinke, Joana Costa. *Europe*. New York: Children's Press, 2019.

Williams, Heather. *Soccer: A Guide for Players and Fans*. North Mankato, MN: Capstone, 2020.

INTERNET SITES

Britannica Kids: England

kids.britannica.com/kids/article/England/353101

English Heritage Kids: Kings and Queens of England

english-heritage.org.uk/members-area/kids/kids-rule-guide
-to-kings-and-queens/

National Geographic Kids: United Kingdom

kids.nationalgeographic.com/geography/countries/article
/united-kingdom

INDEX

ABOUT THE AUTHOR

Nancy Dickmann grew up reading encyclopedias for fun, and after many years working in children's publishing, she now has her dream job as a full-time author. She has had over 200 titles published so far, mainly on science topics, and finds that the best part of the job is researching and learning new things. One highlight was getting to interview a real astronaut to find out about using the toilet in space!

OTHER BOOKS IN THIS SERIES

YOUR PASSPORT TO ARGENTINA
YOUR PASSPORT TO AUSTRALIA
YOUR PASSPORT TO CHINA
YOUR PASSPORT TO ECUADOR
YOUR PASSPORT TO EGYPT
YOUR PASSPORT TO EL SALVADOR
YOUR PASSPORT TO ETHIOPIA
YOUR PASSPORT TO FRANCE
YOUR PASSPORT TO GUATEMALA
YOUR PASSPORT TO IRAN

YOUR PASSPORT TO ITALY
YOUR PASSPORT TO KENYA
YOUR PASSPORT TO MEXICO
YOUR PASSPORT TO PERU
YOUR PASSPORT TO RUSSIA
YOUR PASSPORT TO SOUTH KOREA
YOUR PASSPORT TO SPAIN
YOUR PASSPORT TO SRI LANKA
YOUR PASSPORT TO TURKEY